IMAGES
of America

WAKEFIELD

This edition is dedicated to the late Capt. Richard Brown of the South Kingston Police Department, who dearly loved Wakefield, its people and its history.

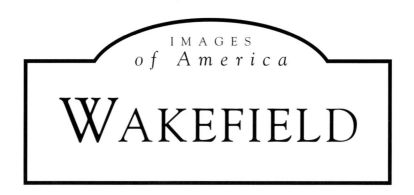

IMAGES
of America

WAKEFIELD

Betty J. Cotter

ARCADIA

First published 1997
Copyright © Betty J. Cotter, 1997

ISBN 0-7524-0863-1

Published by Arcadia Publishing,
an imprint of the Chalford Publishing Corporation,
One Washington Center, Dover, New Hampshire 03820.
Printed in Great Britain

Library of Congress Cataloging-in-Publication Data applied for

Contents

Acknowledgments

The author owes a deep debt of gratitude to the many organizations and individuals who shared their photographs, expertise, and time to make this book possible. I have been overwhelmed by the outpouring of support for this project.

First, I must thank Marc Archambault, Cecilia A. Boggs, and Betty Albro of the Pettaquamscutt Historical Society. Marc early on convinced the society to share its photographs with me, without which this book would not have been possible. Mrs. Boggs, the executive director, and Miss Albro, the curator, generously helped me find materials.

I also owe deep thanks to South Kingstown Library Director Connie Lachowicz and the research staff of Peace Dale Library, which loaned me fifteen pictures for this project. Most of the research for the captions was done in the library's Rhode Island Room.

I also wish to thank Marybeth Reilly McGreen for coming up with the idea for this book and for helping me in the early stages.

I am indebted to the following for proofreading help: Diane Smith, State Rep. Leona A. Kelley, Marjorie Andre, Audrey Hosley, Betty Tucker, and Dennis Bougie, president of the Pettaquamscutt Historical Society.

For their donations of photographs, I wish to thank: Donald and Shirley Southwick, Audrey H. Hosley, Betty Tucker, Shirley Tucker, Robert H. Eaton, David Gates, Arthur Dexter, John L. Sheldon III, Bill Rose, Henry Almonte, retired, Capt. Richard Brown of the South Kingstown Police Department, retired Chief of Police Clinton E. Salisbury Sr., Frank W. Smith Jr., Thelma Gardner, LeRoy B. and Eleanor Kenyon, Everett Stedman, Doug Huber, Annemarie Maccalous of South County Hospital, Peter Gardiner of the South County Museum, Jane E. Costanza, Robert and Diane Smith, Bob Toth, Jim Fleming, Martha Badigian, Marjorie Andre, Everett Hopkins, and Helen Farrell Allen of Tempus Fugit.

I owe special thanks to Audrey Hosley, Edna Otto, Shirley and Donald Southwick, Annemarie Maccalous, and Clinton E. Salisbury Sr. for help in preparing captions. I also am appreciative of support from Laura Kelly of *The Narragansett Times* and Gerry Goldstein of *The Providence Journal* for publicizing this project.

Introduction

This is not a complete history of Wakefield, nor is it even a chronological one. It is impressionistic rather than scholarly, a series of photographs grouped together to give both stranger and resident a better feel for the history and traditions of the village. It is hoped that the reader will come away with a better appreciation for the historic sites that have been preserved, and perhaps regret for those that have not.

Wakefield is not a town; it is a village in the town of South Kingstown, and as such its history is intricately woven with the villages that surround it. The author made a conscious decision not to include many Peace Dale landmarks in this volume because Peace Dale developed separately, has a distinct history, and should be treated perhaps in its own book. To separate the two, the author used the boundaries to the north—the intersection of Church and Columbia Streets and the intersection of Allen Avenue and High Street; Point Judith Pond is Wakefield's southern boundary. A few settlements—such as Tuckertown—were included in this volume because of their many connections with Wakefield. Such areas would not stand on their own, but deserve mention. Occasionally the author has strayed toward the Peace Dale boundary, such as with Broad Rock Farm, but there was always a thematic reason for doing so.

Turn the pages, then, and step back into Wakefield's past. In its strong community ties and lively mercantile tradition may we find the keys to our future.

Betty J. Cotter
Wakefield, Rhode Island

One
School Days

Schoolchildren in South Kingstown portray George and Martha Washington in this 1896 photo. Tableau—the representation of characters or a scene by actors who remain silent—was a popular activity in the late nineteenth century. (Courtesy Pettaquamscutt Historical Society)

South Kingstown High School's Class of 1900 poses on the edge of a new century. The class graduation was a week-long affair that featured a special sermon at Peace Dale Congregational Church and an alumni reception. The graduates were (from left to right) Carolyn Louise Johnson, Helen Elizabeth Peck, Alice Partelow Sheldon, Maude Virginia Champlin, Florence Melissa Barrows, and Walter Sheldon Rodman. Miss Sheldon spoke on "The Modern Education of Women" and Rodman on "Electricity as a Form of Energy" at commencement, held June 28, 1900. (Courtesy Pettaquamscutt Historical Society)

Maude Virginia Champlin took the business course at South Kingstown High School, graduating in 1900. She read the class history at the alumni reception, which was held the evening of commencement in Memorial Hall. (Courtesy Pettaquamscutt Historical Society)

W.R. Jones, principal of South Kingstown High School (now Hazard School), proudly shows off the building at Columbia and School Streets. Designed by Clarke, Howe, and Homer, the distinctive high school was dedicated in 1911 and used as a high school until the present building opened in 1954. For years thereafter it housed fifth- and sixth-graders; today it is a kindergarten center. (Courtesy Pettaquamscutt Historical Society)

This high school was originally located at Columbia and School Streets, until it was moved farther down School Street in 1910 to make way for the new high school, now Hazard School. The above building, dedicated in 1880, replaced a high school that had burned that same year. Today this building sports a second and third story and is the School Street Apartments. (Courtesy Pettaquamscutt Historical Society)

This view of the high school is at its original location at Columbia and School Streets. (Courtesy Pettaquamscutt Historical Society)

These Wakefield Grammar School students are shown about 1897 when the school was located on Main Street in Wakefield, where the Markarian & Meehan Building is now. The teacher, Mary E. Bliss, taught second grade and earned $37.50 a month to teach fifty-three pupils, according to the report of the school committee that year. (Courtesy Pettaquamscutt Historical Society)

These are Wakefield Grammar School students. Beginning shortly after the turn of the century, South Kingstown was moving toward rural school consolidation, closing one-room schools and moving students to larger schools. In the 1914 school committee report, it was noted that within eleven years the town had closed the Tower Hill, Sugar Loaf, and Mooresfield schools and moved those pupils to the Peace Dale, Wakefield, and Kingston schools. Others in the West Kingston and Matunuck areas were closed as well. (Courtesy Pettaquamscutt Historical Society)

These students attended South Kingstown High School in 1898. (Courtesy Pettaquamscutt Historical Society)

14

This is the Wakefield Grammar School Class of 1914 graduates. The front row includes (from left to right) Robert Gillies, Benjamin Shaw, Harry Noka, Mrs. Esther Shannon (teacher), George Watson, and Bert Edwards. The remaining identifications are unclear, but the graduates also included Shirley Pelkey, Marguerite Raitano, Hazel Eccleston, Elizabeth Whaley, Leila Sweet, Pearl Potter, Ruth Hall, Nathalie Pierce, Amy Northrup, Marian Bedard, Catherine Quinn, Helen Lockwood, Ethel Seymour, and Beth Brown. (Courtesy Pettaquamscutt Historical Society)

This is another photograph of the Wakefield Grammar School on Main Street in Wakefield, located where the Markarian & Meehan Building is now. Built as a two-room school in 1849, the school was moved and four rooms added to it thirty years later. When a new grammar school was built in 1908, contractor Louis F. Bell acquired this building and moved it across the street, where it would house a Chinese restaurant and bowling alley on the first floor and the Royal Theatre on the second floor. The building, eventually razed, stood where the entrance to the merchants' parking lot off Main Street is now. (Courtesy Bob and Diane Smith)

Wakefield Grammar School students moved to this site off High Street when this building was constructed in 1908. The Rev. J.W. Fobes, a member of the school committee and pastor of Peace Dale Congregational Church, had the pedestrian footbridge built at his personal expense that same year. It later was rebuilt, and schoolchildren still use it to bike and walk to school. (Courtesy David Gates)

Wakefield Grammar School was destroyed in March 1963 by a blaze believed to have been started by faulty wiring on the auditorium stage. When built in 1908, the school helped the community fulfill its mission of rural school consolidation. Superintendent Bernon Helme believed the benefits of this system to be: more comfortable schoolhouses and equipment, safer transportation, larger and more regular attendance, and "protection of the children from the danger of offenses against good morals, so often the case where pupils go to and from school unaccompanied by some adult." (Courtesy Pettaquamscutt Historical Society)

Like many of South Kingstown's villages, the hamlet of Tuckertown was served by a one-room school. This school was built about 1840 and moved from a wooded area off Worden's Pond Road to this site, near the Tuckertown Four Corners, about 1907. The old location was "a difficult place for the uninitiated to find and inaccessible for the school population of that community," wrote Superintendent Bernon E. Helme in his 1907 report. This school is now a private residence abutting Tuckertown Park. (Courtesy Betty Tucker)

The students of Tuckertown School were mostly Tuckers—and even those with different last names were related to one another. This photo from 1915 shows, from left to right: (front row) Ella Cook, Viola Tucker, Pearl Tucker, Mattie Brayman, and Marion L. Tucker; (back row) James Tucker, Jennie Anna Webster, Everett Webster, Samuel E. Tucker, Ruth Tucker, and George W. Tucker. Siblings were: Jim, Ruth, Viola, and Pearl; Anna and Everett; and Sam, George, and Marion. The teacher, not shown, was C. Elsie Albro of Peace Dale. She made $425 a year. (Courtesy Betty Tucker)

18

The Tuckertown School in winter could be a foreboding place. The school closed for two years during World War I, from 1917 to 1919, because the district couldn't find a teacher. In the bitter cold winter of 1918–19, students were taken to Wakefield Grammar School by horse-drawn wagon. For many, the 4-mile ride to school was preceded by a walk of more than a mile to meet the wagon at Tuckertown Four Corners. (Courtesy Betty Tucker)

School girls relax outside the Wakefield Grammar School in 1943. This view was taken from the field south of the school. (Courtesy Marjorie Tucker Andre)

Graduates of Wakefield Grammar School, Class of 1952, gather for a class portrait. They would eventually attend the new high school, built two years later. Graduations were held in the auditorium of Hazard Memorial Hall. (Courtesy Peace Dale Library)

Two
Good Sports

The 1915–16 South Kingstown High School (SKHS) baseball team poses in front of the school. They are, from left to right: (front row) Ben Shaw, John Degan, and Eddie Wright; (middle row) Arthur Miller, Walt Seymour, Earl Hoyt, and "Copper" Hoyt; (back row) George Watson, Murray Gates, Jack Albro, Henry Tyler, and Fred Coggeshall. (Courtesy Pettaquamscutt Historical Society)

This South Kingstown High School baseball team included, from left to right, (front row) Ray Chappell, Leo Monahan, Isaac Hoyt, George Trimble, Russell Barber; (middle row) Everett Bateman; (top row) Howard Laity, John Primo, Albert Weibel, Leonard S. Holley, Andrew Redmond, and adviser Alfred Maryott. Holley was the team captain. The team was "practically all raw material" and suffered "owing to rain and bad grounds," noted the 1912 *Cryptic*, a SKHS publication. Their record: 6 wins and 14 losses. (Courtesy Pettaquamscutt Historical Society)

This is the South Kingstown High School baseball team in 1909. Three years earlier, principal Horace Mason Hovey had described his philosophy on sports thus: "Athletics is strongly upheld so far as it does not interfere with the success of the student, and an endeavor is constantly made to keep it on a high moral plane." (Courtesy Pettaquamscutt Historical Society)

South Kingstown High School also fielded a track team (date unknown) that included, from left to right, (kneeling) Ray Holley and Tom Connor and (back row) George Holley, George Scott, Jack Scott, principal W.R. Jones, Carl Wheeler, Wilfred Easterbrooks, and Carl Congdon. (Courtesy Pettaquamscutt Historical Society)

In 1920–21, South Kingstown had a semi-professional basketball team. They were, from left to right: (top row) Walter E. Seymour, Thomas F. O'Brien, and James E. Sykes Jr.; (bottom) Leo Martin, Jimmie Kinney, Clifford H. Wilbur, Jimmie Nigrelli, Elmer Sweet, and mascot Frankie Martella. Nigrelli was the captain and manager. (Courtesy Pettaquamscutt Historical Society)

The South Kingstown Rangers were the Southern Rhode Island League champions in 1947 and 1948. This team photo shows, from left to right, (front row) William James, Harvey Weibel, Atmore Fayerweather, George Benson, and John Toth; (second row) Harry Hunt, William Mitchell, Wes Lessard, and an unidentified man; (back row): Clinton Salisbury Sr., Eugene Malgieri, and Emrico DeSista. Among the teams they played were Ashaway, Hope Valley, North Kingstown, East Greenwich, and Narragansett. (Courtesy Clinton Salisbury Sr.)

Three
Days of Rest

The Girls Friendly Society of the Church of the Ascension was a social organization for female members of the Episcopal church on Main Street. In 1920, the girls held their annual dance at Bell's Hall and danced to the music of Main's Orchestra. (Courtesy Pettaquamscutt Historical Society)

Robert Walker and friends gather for a circus about 1895. Admission to the "Big Show" was a nickel. Little else is known about this photo, but it may relate to the circuses that were held in Wakefield at what is now Belmont Shoppers Park. (Courtesy Pettaquamscutt Historical Society)

This party was held at William H. Robinson's home on Kenyon Avenue in the 1890s. Note the boys' knee-pants, a standard of the day. (Courtesy Pettaquamscutt Historical Society)

This Episcopal church was located on Cemetery Lane, now Johnson Place, and was a forerunner to the Church of the Ascension on Main Street. The building, dating to about 1840, was sold in 1879; it is no longer standing. (Courtesy Pettaquamscutt Historical Society)

Church of the Ascension, Wakefield, R. I.

The Church of the Ascension on Main Street was built in 1883 to replace a wooden structure on Cemetery Lane (as seen in the top photograph). The new Episcopal church was constructed from stone salvaged from the Rodman mill at Rocky Brook that had burned. (Courtesy Donald and Shirley Southwick)

St. Francis Church on High Street was originally this wooden structure located next to the parsonage. Initially a Baptist church, the building was torn down after a granite structure at the adjacent corner of Winter and High Streets was built. (Courtesy Pettaquamscutt Historical Society)

The Christ United Methodist Church, the spire of which can be seen in the right of this photograph of Columbia Street, was built about 1890. Today the congregation has moved to a new church on Kingstown Road, Kingston, and the building houses an architect's office. (Courtesy Pettaquamscutt Historical Society)

Wakefield Baptist Church and its parsonage on Main Street is shown here sometime after 1891, when the entrance to the church was changed to the right. The church was built in 1852 at a cost of $8,000, replacing another church dating to 1831 that was moved from the site. In 1853, Henry Jackson reported to the Baptist State Convention that "It is decidedly the best house which I visited in the south part of the State. There are 92 pews, seating 600, which is the number of the congregation, averaging 400." (Courtesy Pettaquamscutt Historical Society)

The cars in this photo of the Wakefield Baptist Church places it in the 1920s. Note the trees in the foreground, which were replaced at some point by flowering cherry. The posts, for tying up horses, are still there. (Courtesy Pettaquamscutt Historical Society)

The fruit counters of the First National Store on Main Street, Wakefield, overflow with bounty in this 1935 photo. The clerks are, from left to right: Alfred Joyal, George Cuttings, and LeRoy B. Kenyon. It was common for the fruit clerks to carry shoppers' purchases to their cars, because the fruit display was the last stop in the store. Mr. Joyal and Mr. Cuttings are deceased; Mr. Kenyon is retired after a long career with the supermarket chain, which eventually moved to Heritage Mall in the Dale Carlia Corner area. (Courtesy LeRoy and Eleanor Kenyon)

Four

The Corner Store

This building at 355 Main Street, Wakefield, typifies the history of Wakefield in that it has housed many retail establishments over the years. Today it is owned by South County Hospital and leased by Olde Friends Antiques; many may remember it as a sort of annex to Kenyon's Department Store over the years, housing the Fannie B. Grafton clothing store. (Courtesy David Gates)

The H.W. Partelow Building, at the corner of Columbia and Main Streets, is today the home of the Italian Village restaurant; this photo was taken about 1882. In 1920 H.W. Partelow still advertised "seed potatoes direct" from Aroostook County, Maine and sold everything from sheep manure to wallpaper. According to the town's 1910 city directory, H.W. Partelow also sold groceries from the site at one time. (Courtesy Bill Rose)

George Babcock is reputed to be the first to sell ice cream in Wakefield from this boarding house, which was located about where the Bell Block is now. In 1899, A.T. Babcock advertised in *The Narragansett Times* "ice cream, water ices and sherbets in any quantities." (Courtesy Pettaquamscutt Historical Society)

Maine's I Scream, located at the southeast point of Dale Carlia Corner, was established in 1884 by W.G. Maine. Maine's delivery wagons were made by Charles H. Armstrong and Sons on Main Street. (Courtesy Frank W. Smith Jr.)

A new conveyance had arrived on the scene by the time this picture was taken at Maine's I Scream on Kingstown Road. In April 1906, W.G. Maine pledged to his patrons in the columns of *The Narragansett Times* that he would not increase the price of his ice cream "until he has consumed the two hundred and forty tons of ice he cut the past winter." (Courtesy Frank W. Smith Jr.)

Delivery trucks were a permanent way of doing business by the time this photo was taken. In the summer of 1935, Maine's I Scream advertised a gallon of ice cream, any flavor, for $1.50, and boasted in a *Narragansett Times* advertisement: "Our factory and retail shoppe are always open until 12 p.m. Plenty of lighted parking space for customers." (Courtesy Frank W. Smith Jr.)

This cinderblock structure was a fixture at Dale Carlia Corner until it was taken down in the 1990s to make way for more Bess Eaton parking. Maine's ceased making ice cream in 1986, one hundred and two years after it opened. (Courtesy Frank W. Smith Jr.)

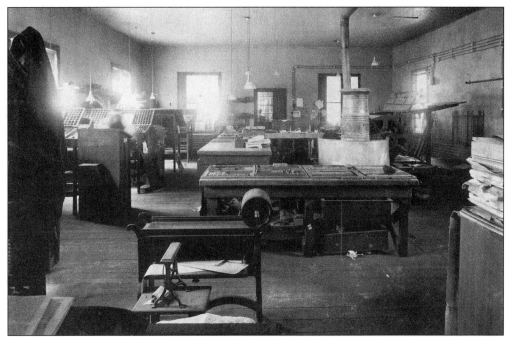

This is the production room of *The Narragansett Times* during the days of hot lead printing. D. Gillies' Sons ran the newspaper until 1946, when Frederick J. Wilson Jr. bought the paper with the help of a loan from John F. Kennedy; the Wilson family owned the paper until it was sold to a chain in 1984. (Courtesy Pettaquamscutt Historical Society)

The What Cheer Laundry, shown here in the summer of 1915, was located near what is now Rawling's Floor Coverings. In the 1910 city directory, What Cheer promised to deliver "that pleasing flexible finish" produced "by washing in nine different clear waters, the use of absolutely pure wheat starch, carefully rubbed in by hand, and expert hand-flat table ironers." B.C. Wilcox was the Wakefield agent for the company, which was based in Providence. (Courtesy Pettaquamscutt Historical Society)

The Saugatucket River was the hub of manufacturing in Wakefield, and the Wakefield Mill at High and Main Streets was one of a cluster of mills that sprang up along the river. The wooden building at the left foreground is gone, but the other two in this photograph are still standing. (Courtesy Pettaquamscutt Historical Society)

Sheldon's Furniture has been an imposing presence on Main Street since the building was moved to the site in 1899 (see Chapter 4). Note the building at the left, also shown at the start of this chapter, which was home to an apothecary. (Courtesy John Sheldon III)

Now the home of Damon's Hardware on Main Street, this three-story bank building on the shores of the Saugatucket River dates to 1889. The bank was home to the Wakefield Institution for Savings from 1904 to 1927. The third floor was lost to a fire on March 24, 1924, that was thought to have originated in the chimney; Narragansett firefighter Osse Cantara was injured when the fire truck in which he was riding overturned. (Courtesy Donald and Shirley Southwick)

The Wakefield Trust Co., founded in 1890, moved to this site on Main Street in the 1920s. The building, which housed the Industrial National Bank in later years, was distinguished by its high ceilings and long windows. In recent years the interior was remodeled for office use, and today it is known as the Markarian & Meehan Building. (Courtesy Donald and Shirley Southwick)

Fleming's Department Store was founded in 1937 by Hayden J. Fleming. At first it was two smaller stores, one dry goods, one clothing; Fleming's then evolved into a department store in the five-and-dime tradition, with wooden floors and bins of merchandise. This store, at what is now Wild Child and Ginger's Cafe and Bakery, closed in 1973, five years after Fleming opened a second store in the Chariho Shopping Plaza in Wyoming, Rhode Island. (Courtesy Jim Fleming)

J.C. Tucker Jr. sold everything from lumber to farm machinery in these buildings. They were located where the Narragansett Pier Railroad crossed Main Street, thus the name "Wakefield Branch" came to describe the store. The store, now owned by Arnold Lumber Co. of West Kingston, will forever be known as "the Branch" to locals. (Courtesy Pettaquamscutt Historical Society)

This commercial block on Robinson Street housed the Colonial Restaurant, among other businesses. Note the Gulf gas station at the far right. The block was razed a few years after this picture was taken in 1933 to make way for the Wakefield Post Office. (Courtesy Pettaquamscutt Historical Society)

The Wakefield Post Office, built in 1936, replaced the commercial block on Robinson Street (above). The building is distinguished by a mural of the Narragansett Planters painted by WPA artist Ernest Hamlin Baker. (Courtesy Robert H. Eaton)

Wright's Opera House, the larger of the two buildings to the right, was the center of the community's entertainment. Silas Wright built Wright's Hall in 1882 after a blaze at Columbia Hall (where the *Narragansett Times* is now) took out most of the surrounding buildings. The building, by then called Wright's Opera House, was struck by another fire in 1918. (Courtesy Bob and Diane Smith)

The Community Theatre, which took the place of Wright's Opera House on Columbia Street, was located where Campus Cinema is today. First-run movies preceded by the inevitable cartoon short and news reel were the movie house's main fare. This is a still from a movie shot by a Community Theatre cameraman in the 1930s. (Courtesy David Gates)

Five

Main Street

It's the little nuances that people love about Main Street, such as this tree that once graced the intersection of Main and High Streets. In recent years a traffic circle of marigolds replaced the tree. Despite many changes over the decades, businesses and homeowners along the stretch still strive to beautify downtown with flowers and artful displays of merchandise. (Courtesy Pettaquamscutt Historical Society)

An elegant country inn at the base of Sugar Loaf Hill is one of Main Street's first noticed landmarks. The Larchwood Inn, built in 1831 by Wakefield Mill owner James Robinson, was known first as "The Larches" for the trees on the property. Another Wakefield Mill owner, Stephen Wright, extensively remodeled the building in the 1850s. It first opened as the Larchwood Inn in 1926 and continues as a restaurant and inn today. (Courtesy Donald and Shirley Southwick)

The view down Sugar Loaf Hill remains as scenic as in this postcard, and the wall to the left—in front of the Larchwood Inn—is still standing. (Courtesy Pettaquamscutt Historical Society)

The Sylvester Robinson Store, now Point Jude Boats, is the lighter colored building on the left. Mr. Robinson built the store in 1846 and lived in the building at the extreme left. He also served as president of the Wakefield Bank, which was located across the street from his house in a stone building not visible in this photo. (Courtesy Bob and Diane Smith)

The bank building that is now Damon's Hardware also housed the Rhode Island Militia, the Loyal Order of Moose, doctors' offices, and a dentist's office. Note the tree and water fountain in this photo, taken from the High Street intersection. (Courtesy Pettaquamscutt Historical Society)

The Saugatucket River was first dammed some time before 1850, creating hydropower for the various versions of the Wakefield Mill. Mill buildings are to the right in this photo and the three-story bank building on Main Street is in the rear left. Note how dry the Saugatucket River is. (Courtesy Henry Almonte)

The Wakefield House stood on the southern side of Main Street, near what is now the entrance to McGrath's Package Store. (Courtesy Bob and Diane Smith)

Babcock's Boarding House and Livery Stable was first located near where the Bell Block is now. The building was moved across the street to become part of the Wakefield House before 1890 and was burned in 1969 to make way for McGrath's Package Store. (Courtesy David Gates)

In this postcard, postmarked 1908, the horse and carriage was still the main form of Main Street travel. This view was taken looking north; the Wakefield Baptist Church can be seen in the far skyline. (Courtesy Robert H. Eaton)

Kenyon's Department Store, shown at right, dominated the Main Street mercantile scene for 139 years before closing in October 1996. An old-fashioned department store, it was established in 1857 by William G. Kenyon and remained in the same family until its closing. The building shown here was built in 1891 and is now owned by South County Hospital, which uses it to sell surgical supplies. This postcard is postmarked 1905. (Courtesy Robert H. Eaton)

The Church of the Ascension, in the far right corner of this photograph, dates the photo to at least the 1890s, probably the turn of the century. Look closely and you will see two women walking in ankle-length dresses near Kenyon Avenue. (Courtesy Pettaquamscutt Historical Society)

At the intersection of Robinson and Main Streets, passengers on the Narragansett Pier Railroad could look out their train car windows and know immediately where they were by the stone markings on the hill next to the station. Aside from the loss of the house on the hill above the sign and the demise of the railroad, little has changed in this view of Main Street. (Courtesy Peace Dale Library)

In 1899, using only oxen and manpower, a man named Thomas Sweeney of Providence began a massive undertaking: moving the John L. Sheldon furniture company down Main Street from its home near what is now Johnson Place to a new spot next to the Bell Block. The move took three weeks, and historian Oliver Stedman recalled people driving their wagons beneath the jacked-up building. (Courtesy John L. Sheldon III)

The John L. Sheldon furniture company is shown here at its first home west of the Saugatucket River bridge, probably in the 1860s. The building, which withstood a move in 1899, still stands today and is run by a descendent of its founder. (Courtesy John L. Sheldon III)

The Sheldon building is backed into its new home opposite Kenyon's Department Store (see awnings, right). The building was raised and a new, first story erected beneath it. (Courtesy John L. Sheldon III)

This postcard, postmarked 1942 but possibly made in the 1930s, shows the First National Store in a one-story building. The store moved to the site from another Main Street location in 1934. Note the angled parking on the north side of the street. (Courtesy Robert H. Eaton)

A still from the movie *It's a Holiday*, shot by a cameraman from the Community Theatre, shows the Wakefield Diner, a trolley-car-type diner run by Berry Whiting. In 1935, about the time this was filmed, Whiting proclaimed in the South Kingstown High School yearbook, *The Anchor*: "Table and Counter Service. Good Food Well Served." (Courtesy David Gates)

The C.H. Armstrong & Sons Carriage Works, located about where South County Motors is now, was the site of a large carriage manufacturing operation that also included a warehouse on Woodruff Avenue. The carriage works had its beginnings in 1861 and closed in 1921, when its attempts to enter the automobile business failed. (Courtesy Bob and Diane Smith)

To the left in this view of Main Street can be seen the Nathaniel G. Armstrong House, now home to H.D. Randall Realtors, and the John Armstrong House. Nathaniel Armstrong built the first carriages in town; John was his brother. (Courtesy Pettaquamscutt Historical Society)

COLUMBIA HOUSE.

WAKEFIELD, R. I.

Guests are hereby notified that the Proprietor will not be responsible for Valuables, Money, Jewelry, Etc., unl[...]
posited in the Safe at the Office.   W. B. DAVIDSON, Prop[...]

Name.	Residence.	Time.	Room.	Horse
ONE Night Only "Widow Bedott" Co. OPERA HOUSE Saturday Night — DEC 27th				

This ledger from the Columbia House, known also as the Armstrong House, shows that the actors playing at the nearby Wright Opera House often stayed at the hotel, located at the intersection of Main Street and Woodruff Avenue. The building is home today to W.E. Stedman Co., a bike shop. (Courtesy Bob and Diane Smith)

The home of Duncan Gillies was located directly across from his business, *The Narragansett Times*. Years later this house was moved to make way for a gas station, and it still stands unoccupied on Woodruff Avenue. Note the imposing pine trees that are long gone. The Gillies family built several houses on Woodruff Avenue, including two beautiful Victorians, for the Gillies' sons. (Courtesy Pettaquamscutt Historical Society)

The Columbia House's first floor became home to Archie Brown's motorcycle and bicycle dealership, which had been in a barn behind Brown's parents' house on Robinson Street, in the 1920s. This photo shows Brown (left), an unidentified worker (behind doorway), and William E. Stedman. Shortly after this photo was taken, Brown died of pneumonia and the worker (center) drowned in Silver Lake, according to Stedman's son, Everett Stedman. W. Luther Bates, who ran the stove shop in the adjacent space, also died suddenly while walking up Main Street. (Courtesy Everett Stedman)

Looking west, this photo shows Archie Brown's bicycle and motorcycle shop (at left) and *The Narragansett Times* office (extreme right). (Courtesy Pettaquamscutt Historical Society)

The residence of George H. Sheldon, this house appears to be similar to the Victorian building at 105 Main Street. The decorative wall remains. (Courtesy Donald and Shirley Southwick)

Six

Dale Carlia Corner

Forever gone, this is the Dale Carlia Corner that was paved over beginning in the 1950s. This peaceful scene was photographed from the property of Twin Chimneys, a stately farmhouse owned by the Holley family near what is now Benny's Home and Auto Store and Holley Street. (Courtesy Audrey H. Hosley)

In 1927, the intersection of Dale Carlia Corner was wide but nearly deserted. This was the edge of town, not the center of it, and even though Route 1 passed right through town via Main Street and Old Tower Hill Road, traffic was minimal. This view is looking east; note that Route 108 was then known as Route 107 and Route 1-A was 1-B. (Courtesy Robert H. Eaton)

Taken at the same time as the above photograph—April 22, 1927—this view is looking west along Old Tower Hill Road toward Main Street. Observe the neighborhood of houses at the left, what is now Belmont Shoppers Park. (Courtesy Robert H. Eaton)

Twin Chimneys was the name of this farmhouse located on a gentle rise behind what is now Benny's Home and Auto Store. The home of George A. and Lillian Elnora (Tucker) Holley, it was razed in 1957 so the Roger Williams Savings and Loan Association could build a bank building on the site. The house dated to at least 1714, possibly as early as 1693, and had been restored by the Holley family when they bought it in 1913. Rowland Hazard owned the property from 1819 until his death in 1838, and it is said that he dubbed the area "Dale Carlia" after visiting that region of Sweden, for it reminded him of that gently rolling country. This view is from the west side of what is now Oak Street. (Courtesy Audrey Hosley)

This house on Main Street, also in the Holley family, was torn to make way for Belmont Shoppers Park. Audrey (Holley) Hosley, who grew up in the house, remembers watching from the A&P (now Fleet Bank) as the wrecking ball smashed into her bedroom. (Courtesy Audrey Hosley)

Twin Chimneys from Main Street in January 1945 presented a tranquil vista. When the house was demolished in 1957, construction crews removed 20,000 yards of gravel from the sloping house site. (Courtesy Audrey Hosley)

Holley's Inc. held school bus contracts and did trucking to Providence, New London, and other parts of Connecticut. Originally called the Holley Ice Co., and at one time the Holley Ice and Transportation Co., the company was started in the 1920s by George A. Holley and taken over by his sons in 1937. The company's trucks and bus make an impressive scene in this photograph, which shows the houses on Cherry Lane that were moved or destroyed when Belmont Shoppers Park was built. (Courtesy Audrey Hosley)

The employees of Holley's Inc. pose in front of their office on Kingstown Road at Dale Carlia Corner. They are, from left to right: Alice King Davidson, Leonard Holley (part-owner), Margaret Brown (part-owner), Audrey Holley Hosley, David Sherman, and Carleton Brown. (Courtesy Audrey Hosley)

The Holley business was multi-faceted, as shown by this sign on the building at Dale Carlia Corner. (Courtesy Audrey Hosley)

This Sunoco station, at the foreground of what is now the Dale Carlia Shopping Center parking lot, was owned by the Holley Ice and Transportation Co. Louis M. Gates, shown here, ran the station; he was married to Harriet Holley Gates. (Courtesy Audrey Hosley)

This photo was taken in August 1955, about the time the A&P was built on the northeast corner of the Dale Carlia intersection. The former Sunoco station in the top photo can be seen in this photo at the site to which it had been moved. The building would be moved again to behind A&P (by then Fleet Bank) before being demolished. (Courtesy Jane Costanza)

This is a picture of the A&P around the time it opened in August 1955. The car in the foreground is from a much earlier time. Note the prices in the windows—steaks were just 89¢ a pound. In an advertisement in *The Narragansett Times* on August 11, 1955, a week after its grand opening, A&P boasted of its "streamlined self-service features—the spacious parking area—the convenient parcel pickup service . . ." The manager was Martin Ballou. (Courtesy Jane Costanza)

This block of stores at the Dale Carlia Shopping Center opened in 1957. Dale Carlia Corner would soon develop in all directions, with the Quo Vadis Shopping Center built on Kingstown Road in 1958 and Almacs supermarket across the street from Quo Vadis in 1964. (Courtesy Jane Costanza)

The Holley family is seen here outside Twin Chimneys, the farm at Dale Carlia Corner, after purchasing it in 1913. The house was built to last centuries, but it could not withstand the forces of progress. When it was demolished, ground quahog shells were found mixed in the chimney's mortar. (Courtesy Audrey Hosley)

Audrey Holley and Roscoe Hosley are pictured here on their wedding day, September 7, 1946, at the Holley residence near what is now Hospital Trust National Bank. Travelers on Route 1 could gas up at the corner on their way out of town, but otherwise the Holleys' neighborhood was a quiet area of flower gardens and farm animals. (Courtesy Audrey Hosley)

This aerial view of the Dale Carlia area, looking southwest toward Salt Pond, was taken sometime after World War II. It shows how little development had occurred in that postwar time. (Courtesy Bob Toth)

Creamery Pond at Old Mountain Field was so named because nearby, about where the Indian Run Village elderly apartments are today, was Mountain Farm Dairy, a creamery run by Irving Yost. Audrey Hosley remembers being told of the dairy dumping skim milk in the pond. (Courtesy Pettaquamscutt Historical Society)

The barns at Broad Rock Farm once were a short distance from Dale Carlia Corner; the next chapter tells more. (Courtesy Audrey Hosley)

Seven

Down on the Farm

Corn-cutting time at Broad Rock Farm required many hands. Broad Rock Farm, located where the St. Dominic Savio Boys Center is now, was a large concern that sold dairy products, produce, and ice. (Courtesy Audrey Hosley)

The Saugatucket Ice Co., part of Broad Rock Farm, was an important link in village merchandising before refrigeration. Ice was cut from Saugatucket Pond. George A. Holley was manager of the farm and its ice plant in 1910, according to the city directory. (Courtesy Audrey Hosley)

The barn here was located at the Hope Jersey Farm on Winter Street in Wakefield. Arthur Dexter resurrected his grandfather's farm, Hope Farm, in 1950 and called it Hope Jersey Farm after the Jersey dairy cows he raised. Off Kenwood Drive, which did not exist then, can be seen one of the farm's silos. The farm closed about 1969–70. (Courtesy Arthur Dexter)

The Broad Rock Farm milkman poses with his horse and wagon. As late as 1935, the farm still sold Grade A raw milk and argued in its advertisements against pasteurization. "Clean milk is always superior to cleaned milk," proclaimed the advertisement in the *Narragansett Times*. (Courtesy Pettaquamscutt Historical Society)

In 1935 Broad Rock Farm was home to 120 head of cattle, which the company boasted were all tuberculin tested and free of disease. The company sold Grade A Guernsey milk and also raised Holsteins at one time. (Courtesy Audrey Hosley)

John Clarke Tucker (1898–1943) shows off his potatoes in this photograph taken by a fertilizer salesman named Al LaPrise. This photo and the one opposite were used to sell fertilizer—and given the yield and size of these spuds, it's easy to see why. Tucker farmed fields located at Tuckertown's sharp curve, near the Wakefield Water Co. well fields. (Courtesy Betty Tucker)

Henry Tucker is shown here with his pride and joy, potatoes. Tucker was among the first to farm potatoes on a large commercial scale in South County, according to his daughter, Marjorie Andre. Note the rows of chicken coops in the background, which belonged to Maurice Tucker. (Courtesy Marjorie Andre)

The picture of this house at Broad Rock Farm was probably taken on a Monday, wash day; witness the clothes blowing in the breeze. (Courtesy Donald and Shirley Southwick)

When Charles W. Tucker built this farmhouse in 1885, it had a walk-in barn below. The house, still standing at 777 Tuckertown Rd., is shown here in a 1946 photo. The Tuckers have raised chickens and grown turf and potatoes in the area for years. (Courtesy Betty Tucker)

This Tucker farmhouse, home to Sam Tucker and also still standing, is shown in a 1911 postcard. Although altered on the western end, it is instantly recognizable to the Tuckertown Road traveler. (Courtesy Betty Tucker)

Roy Dill (left) and Henry Tucker show off a bobcat they shot, apparently in the woods of Tuckertown. Hunting and trapping was an occupation of many farmers. Tucker pulled the trigger. (Courtesy Marjorie Andre)

Marjorie (Tucker) Andre plays with her baby ducks in 1945. Mrs. Andre's father, Henry Tucker, raised chickens and potatoes in his farm on the southern side of Tuckertown Road, across the street from the farm on the bottom of page 72. Note the neat and orderly rows of chicken coops, long since demolished. Marjorie's brother, the late Hollis Tucker, was a potato farmer and champion horse puller. (Courtesy Marjorie Andre)

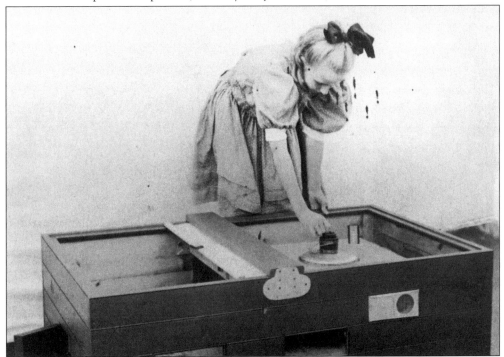

Ina Smith of 43 Whitford Street, later Mrs. Harold L. Salisbury, was about twelve years old when she helped the J.A. Jocoy Co. of Wakefield demonstrate Jocoy's Hygienic Brooder—"The only brooder in the world that can be cared for from the top." (Courtesy Clinton Salisbury Sr.)

Eight

Getting Around

A Narragansett Pier Railroad train clatters over the crossing at the Saugatucket River in Wakefield. Chartered in 1868, the railroad eventually connected Kingston to Narragansett Pier and carried well-heeled travelers to the hotels by the sea. (Courtesy Pettaquamscutt Historical Society)

Engine No. 3, "The Wakefield," of the Narragansett Pier Railroad, was built in 1883. Elisha Gardiner was its engineer. (Courtesy Peace Dale Library)

Within a stone's throw of the Narragansett Pier Railroad tracks was a budding new form of transportation. Archie Brown (left) and William E. Stedman sold Indian motorcycles and bicycles from a barn behind Archie's parents' house at Robinson Street and Woodruff Avenue. This photo was probably taken about 1916, before Brown moved the business to the first floor of Columbia House. (Courtesy Everett Stedman)

Archie Brown and members of an Indian motorcycle club pose outside Brown's shop on Robinson Street. His parents and sister can be seen in the background. This photo was taken about 1915–16. (Courtesy Everett Stedman)

Dr. William Hazard is proudly turned out with his one-horse carriage. Dr. Hazard, who lived on Post Road, poses just east of Columbia Corner, in front of publisher Duncan Gillies' house. Perhaps the portrait was for the newspaper's benefit. (Courtesy Pettaquamscutt Historical Society)

The iron horse would quickly overtake the stage as the transportation of choice for travelers heading to Narragansett Pier for the summer. Ground was broken at Tefft Hill on February 4, 1876, and by July 10, the rails had reached the Pier. This is Engine No. 1, a 4-4-0 Mason. (Courtesy Peace Dale Library)

Engine No. 1, after being rebuilt with an extended smoke box, is shown on the Robinson Street stretch of the Narragansett Pier Railroad line. (Courtesy Peace Dale Library)

The Wakefield Station of the Narragansett Pier Railroad was located at Depot Square, where the line crossed Main Street to Robinson Street. The station, shown here about 1876, was razed in 1948. (Courtesy Peace Dale Library)

The Mickey Dink, a bus that ran on the steel rails of the Narragansett Pier Railroad, was nicknamed for the first names of the men who ran it. This view shows one of the buses in 1921, with (from left to right) Raymond Wright, Francis Cook, and Sprague Sims. The rail buses stopped running in 1952. The railroad line was ripped up in the 1980s, but the state plans to build a bike path along the route. (Courtesy Peace Dale Library)

Nine

Keeping the Peace

Children gather for bicycle inspections in front of the South Kingstown Police Station on Main Street (what is now Universal Firearms). The photo was probably taken about 1944. This building at one time was the station house for the Sea View Railroad. (Courtesy Capt. Richard Brown, SKPD)

Officer Earl Belknap and Police Chief Walter McNulty trade secrets inside the police station on Main Street. McNulty was the town's first police chief, hired as an officer in 1927 and made the first chief in 1931. Belknap, who also served on the town council, designed the interior of this station. (Courtesy Capt. Richard Brown, SKPD)

Officers of the South Kingstown Police Department pose in front of the dispatcher's desk at the police station on Main Street. They are, from left to right: Dan Pucella, Fred Gould, Ronald Hawksley, and Eddie Walsh. The officers sometimes would work a late shift until 2 am, catch a few hours of sleep in the cells, and get up for the 6 am shift. (Courtesy Clinton E. Salisbury Sr.)

Alfred S. Palange proudly shows off a South Kingstown police cruiser in March 1953, outside the police station on Main Street. Palange would rise to the rank of lieutenant. (Courtesy Clinton Salisbury Sr.)

Desk officer and patrolman Everett Emery worked for the University of Rhode Island (then Rhode Island State College) and the South Kingstown Police Department. (Courtesy Clinton E. Salisbury Sr.)

Officer Fred Gould (left) and Chief Walter McNulty investigate a mock crime scene at the Town Hall during a session of the South Kingstown Police School in February 1940. A stuffed dummy was the victim. (Courtesy Capt. Richard Brown, SKPD)

Chief Walter McNulty demonstrates "iodine fuming," a technique of lifting fingerprints. The officer's warm breath would interact with iodine crystals to form a brown gas that reacted with the oil in the fingerprints. (Courtesy Capt. Richard Brown, SKPD)

Officer Peter Costanza and Chief Walter McNulty pose in the "Royal Theatre" on Main Street. Costanza joined McNulty as the town's second police officer in April 1928. McNulty recalled in a 1964 department history how making an arrest was a time-consuming, cumbersome process before he was sworn in as chief. "In case of an intoxicated person, he was usually quite sober by the time we had reached the jail," he wrote in *The Narragansett Times*. (Courtesy Capt. Richard Brown, SKPD)

Also taken in the Royal Theatre, this photograph shows (from left to right) Deputy Chief Peter Costanza, Maurice Marco, Chief Walter McNulty, Joseph Congdon, Fred Gould, and Joseph Flesia. Gould was named deputy chief to succeed Costanza. (Courtesy Capt. Richard Brown, SKPD)

The police reserves, which formed in the late 1940s, included a number of men who eventually became full-time officers. Among those you may recognize in this photo are retired Lt. William Reels, left of the state flag; Al Jansen, to right of state flag; and (kneeling, from left to right) Danny Pucella, Lester Spink, and Arthur Caswell. The reserves have since been disbanded. (Courtesy Capt. Richard Brown, SKPD)

The ground is broken for a new police station to replace the Main Street building. Among those on hand in this 1963–64 photo are, from left to right: Arthur S. Grasso, councilman; unidentified; Dewey Brewster, councilman; unidentified; Alexander M. Cruickshank, council president; retired Police Chief Walter McNulty (with shovel); Police Chief Joseph Congdon; Foster Sheldon, town clerk; and John Hopkins. (Courtesy Capt. Richard W. Brown, SKPD)

The new police station on Route 1 was only one story when it opened in 1964. Soon the town's growing population would necessitate a second story being added to the building. Several other sites were considered for this building, including High Street and Curtis Corner Road. Coincidentally, the town in 1997 is building a new station at the latter site. (Courtesy Capt. Richard Brown, SKPD)

Chief Clinton E. Salisbury Sr. is shown here. In 1964, after being promoted to captain, he told a *Narragansett Times* reporter that he had drawn his gun several times, "and I intended to use it—but it always turned out that I didn't have to." Salisbury was named chief in 1968, replacing Joseph Congdon, and retired in 1981, when he was succeeded by current Chief Vincent Vespia Jr. (Courtesy Clinton E. Salisbury Sr.)

A contingent of police officers march in a parade along Main Street, probably in the 1950s. They had just marched past the Wakefield Branch when this was taken from outside the Main Street police station. (Courtesy Clinton E. Salisbury Sr.)

WAKEFIELD
FIRE DEPT.
1906

The men of the Wakefield Fire Department in 1906 cut imposing figures. Perhaps it was because they had just acquired new uniform patches that year, which *The Narragansett Times* reported were "of a neat design, with the firemen's emblems in the center, and the words 'Wakefield Fire Dept.' at bottom." The department was formed as the Wakefield Hook and Ladder Co. in 1895. (Courtesy Pettaquamscutt Historical Society)

The members of the Wakefield Fire Department are seen here in full dress outside the station on Robinson Street, probably before a parade. The station was built in 1923, replacing the department's first headquarters west of the railroad tracks on Main Street. In 1997 the station is under renovation. (Courtesy Pettaquamscutt Historical Society)

Ten
On the Water

This postcard of Salt Pond, probably made in the late 1930s or early 1940s, shows it was a busy spot even then. The pond is divided between Narragansett and South Kingstown. (Courtesy Robert H. Eaton)

This is another view of Salt Pond, variously called Point Judith Pond, Salt Lake Pond, and Narragansett Lake. Near what is now Stone Cove Marina was called Stone Water Fence Cove because of a stone wall a property owner had erected to keep out fishermen. (Courtesy Bob and Diane Smith)

This is a serene view of Salt Pond. Since the time when the Narragansett Indians were its only denizens, the pond has teemed with oysters, scallops, and other shellfish. Oyster beds started to decline in the 1930s after the pond was breached and upper beds became polluted with sewage. (Courtesy Robert H. Eaton)

Point Judith Pond, Wakefield, R. I.

At one time recreational boaters more or less had Salt Pond to themselves. Before motor cars, motor boats could be seen on the pond, according to historian Oliver H. Stedman. (Courtesy Donald and Shirley Southwick)

The Saugatucket River empties into Salt Pond. This view shows it passing behind Wakefield's commercial district. Although textile mills polluted the water for years, today it is home to a variety of ducks, fish, and turtles, and fishermen have returned to its banks. (Courtesy Donald and Shirley Southwick)

A child along the shores of the Saugatucket appears here in this photograph. (Courtesy Donald and Shirley Southwick)

The Saugatucket River, looking slow and stagnant, wends its way through Wakefield. The spire of the Wakefield Baptist Church can be seen at the right. At one time the river had to be dredged. (Courtesy Donald and Shirley Southwick)

Clark's Cove is seen here at low tide. Note the fishing shacks along the shore, which were a common sight. Although there was a Clarke's Dock in Snug Harbor, Edward L. Coman's map of Salt Pond, first made in 1926, doesn't show a Clark's Cove. (Courtesy Donald and Shirley Southwick)

Silver Lake is seen here when it was the sole province of Shadow Farm, which is visible in the distance in this postcard. (Courtesy Donald and Shirley Southwick)

The Matunuck Beach House in this postcard provided a haven for the weary traveler who wrote on the back in 1929: "Am having just what the doctor told me I must—an absolute rest." Matunuck's frontage on both the ocean and Potter Pond made it an ideal site for several hotels and boarding houses. (Courtesy David Gates)

The summer home of Edward Everett Hale, author of *Man Without a Country*, can still be seen in the Matunuck Hills off Route 1. The cool ocean breezes and rural atmosphere attracted a number of wealthy visitors to the outskirts of Wakefield. (Courtesy David Gates)

Eleven

Patriotic and Community Spirit

The World War II honor roll monument is dedicated in the field next to Wakefield School. The monument was eventually removed and the field, known as Saugatucket Park, now includes a permanent tribute to the town's veterans. (Courtesy Thelma Gardner)

Samuel B.M. Read was one of the many South Kingstown residents who headed south during the Civil War. After enlisting as a first lieutenant in 1861, he was wounded in the Battle of the Wilderness and saw action in Spotsylvania before leaving the armed services in 1864. (Courtesy Doug Huber)

The occasion was the Third Liberty Loan, a bond program to raise money for the World War I effort. A parade to drum up bond sales was a smashing success, the largest parade in the town's history up until that point. The April 6, 1918 event drew 1,100 people to the streets, as estimated in *The Narragansett Times*, and stores and homes were decorated for the occasion. The soldiers included "a battalion of regulars from Fort Kearney." (Courtesy Audrey Hosley)

Lieutenant Johnson keeps his marchers in line during the Third Liberty Loan parade in 1918. They are turning the corner from High Street to Main. The 1918 Liberty Loan campaign took the Liberty Bell as its symbol, and tiny pins with the bell on them were distributed to supporters. "God forbid that the children of those men who rang the Liberty Bell should fail to give dollars, when dollars mean the lives of their own children," went the not-so-subtle appeal in an April 5th *Narragansett Times* advertisement. (Courtesy Audrey Hosley)

This "cage" contained a real person portraying the kaiser, who has been captured at last, in the Third Liberty Loan parade of 1918. The *Narragansett Times* opined: "The goat of the Woodmen of the World and the cage behind the Junior Mechanics float with its black bars and mutes behind, with the 'kaiser' in the cage, was another novel feature." (Courtesy Audrey Hosley)

Dr. Thomas Nestor, who would be a neighborhood physician in Wakefield after World War II, is shown here on the island of New Guinea. This photo was taken about 1943. Note his shaving kit hanging on the palm tree. (Courtesy Martha Badigian)

The battered tea kettles, pots, and pans of many a housewife were melted down for the war effort during World War II. Scrap was collected at two sites in 1942—the state college and town hall—and a Providence junk dealer paid $1,500 for 300 tons. (Courtesy Pettaquamscutt Historical Society)

The South Kingstown Lions Club paper drives were a true community effort, as witnessed by the newspapers collected in this 1940s photograph. The club members are, from left to right: (front row) Elisha Robinson, Firth Rollinson, Charles Barber, Raymond Bressler, Martin Dykstra, and Bill Gates; (back row) Kleber Avery, Fred Wolf, Ted Odland, John Cerwin, George Arnold, Bill Tully, Ben Rose, Arthur Dexter, and Reuben Eaton. (Courtesy David Gates)

This is a parade on Robinson Street. The marchers look like dough boys going off to war, although the date of this photograph is unknown. Note the train waiting at the freight station. (Courtesy Pettaquamscutt Historical Society)

President Franklin D. Roosevelt's National Industrial Recovery Act (NRA), which ensured fair business competition, prompted this celebration in October 1934. The "me" in the photograph is Nina Mellor Hopkins, who worked at the Peace Dale Mill at the time. The NRA would be declared unconstitutional the following year. (Courtesy Everett J. Hopkins)

Twelve
The Best Medicine

South County Hospital on Kenyon Avenue was built in 1924 after the community quickly outgrew a cottage hospital that had been established on the same street. Today numerous additions have turned the hospital into a sprawling complex. (Courtesy Robert H. Eaton)

Bricklayers working for contractor Louis F. Bell erect the walls of South County Hospital on October 11, 1924. "The hospital," wrote *The Narragansett Times*, "occupies the highest point of the old town farm—as sightly a location as could be desired . . ." (Courtesy South County Hospital)

The new hospital, above, with its three stories, was quite a change from the Walter Watson house on Kenyon Avenue that had been the South County Cottage Hospital's first home. Planning for that first hospital began in 1919, after a patient died on the way to Providence. "No one can foresee how it will grow," benefactor Caroline Hazard wrote in her first annual report. (Courtesy South County Hospital)

Dr. John Paul Jones and his wife, Carolyn, relax in the cottage hospital on Kenyon Avenue. They purchased the house after a new hospital was built. Mrs. Jones acted as the cottage hospital's first superintendent. "Her courage and enthusiasm have carried us over many hard places," wrote Caroline Hazard. In its first nine months, the cottage hospital admitted 135 patients, including 88 for surgery. (Courtesy South County Hospital)

Miss Caroline Hazard, essentially the founder of South County Hospital, is shown at a Main Street house with young Red Cross volunteers. They were, from left to right, Margaret Lincoln, an unidentified boy, Margaret Holley, Miss Hazard, Howard Possner, Hilda Northup, Robert Sykes, Ida Lincoln, Jane Kenyon, Etta Phillips, Elinor Hazard, Marjorie Hazard, Madeline Possner, and Jane Taft. The boys and girls helped raise money for the hospital through such efforts as a white elephant table (before which they are shown). (Courtesy South County Hospital)

Dr. John Paul Jones was one of only two doctors in Wakefield for many years. He continued to practice medicine in his eighties and nineties and died six days before his 93rd birthday, in 1980. (Courtesy South County Hospital)

Dr. Henry B. Potter found his first car a much easier way to make house calls than the horse and buggy, which he hated. Dr. Potter and Dr. Jones, related by marriage, were the only two doctors in town when the South County Cottage Hospital was established in 1919. He died in 1958. (Courtesy South County Hospital)

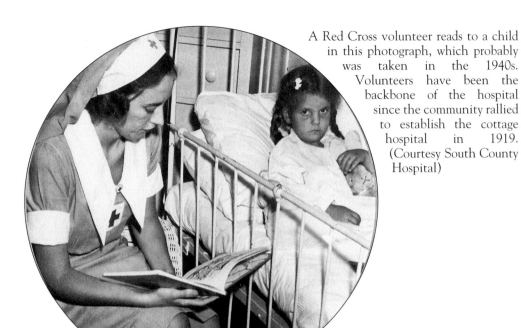

A Red Cross volunteer reads to a child in this photograph, which probably was taken in the 1940s. Volunteers have been the backbone of the hospital since the community rallied to establish the cottage hospital in 1919. (Courtesy South County Hospital)

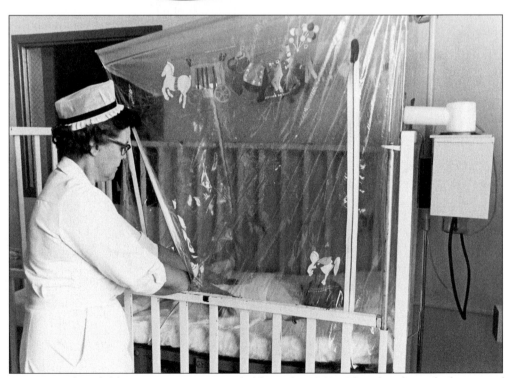

A nurse tends a child in an oxygen tent, probably in the 1960s. That decade marked a time of expansion for the hospital and the addition of specialists to the staff, including a pediatrician. (Courtesy South County Hospital)

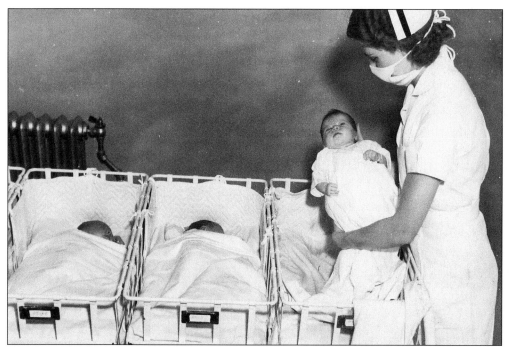

Before the Cottage Hospital was established, women were having their babies at home. By the time the new South County Hospital had been built, women stayed on the first floor while their babies were on the second. Today, the hospital has returned to the past with rooming-in offered to all new mothers. (Courtesy South County Hospital)

Christmas in the hospital can be a lonely time. This photograph, probably from the 1930s, shows Dr. John Paul Jones and South County Hospital nurses helping a young patient celebrate the holiday. (Courtesy South County Hospital)

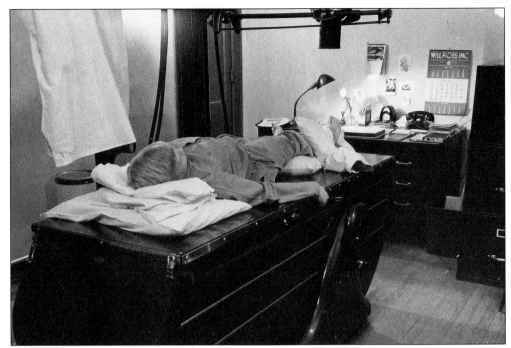

Although the date on the calendar is indecipherable, this photo of South County Hospital's X-ray machine probably dates to the 1940s. Will Ross Inc. was a surgical supply house. (Courtesy South County Hospital)

In the linen room, repairs to johnnies and sheets were made on a sewing machine, shown here in June 1942. (Courtesy South County Hospital)

A nurse prepares medication in this June 1942 photograph. Only nursing supervisors were allowed to dispense medication. That some month, *The Narragansett Times* listed six doctors in town: Dr. S.A. Capalbo, Dr. Clifford Hathaway, Dr. John P. Jones, Dr. A.L. Manganaro, Dr. Henry B. Potter, and Dr. S.J. Turco. (Courtesy South County Hospital)

Dr. Thomas P. Nestor was among several doctors who came to Wakefield after serving in World War II. He practiced general medicine from a white house behind what is now the annex to Damon's Hardware on Main Street. Dr. Nestor was one of the few doctors who continued to make house calls after such a practice had been abandoned by many of his peers. (Courtesy Martha Badigian)

South County Hospital is seen here from the air in this 1964 photo. Note that the road from Bacon House (to left of hospital) had not been built. The photo shows the Hazard Wing to the

right, the hospital's first major addition, which was added in the 1950s and raised the number of beds to sixty-five. (Photo by Robert Wilkie, Courtesy South County Hospital)

Donald L. Ford (second from left), South County Hospital's president from 1958 to 1986, lead the hospital through a period of enormous growth and change, bringing in specialists and expanding hospital facilities. In this 1962 photo, Benjamin R. Sturges, president of the board of trustees, and Ford accept the final Hill-Burton reimbursement for the 1961 addition. Also present are Ernest Cook of the state Department of Health (far left), Gov. John Notte (second from right), and Earl W.G.H. Howard, vice president and treasurer of the hospital board (right). (Courtesy South County Hospital)

Ralph Misto was lured to South County Hospital by President Donald L. Ford in 1966 to head the laboratory. Thirty years later he would retire as hospital president. (Photo by Robert Wilkie, Courtesy South County Hospital)

Thirteen

On the Streets
Where We Live

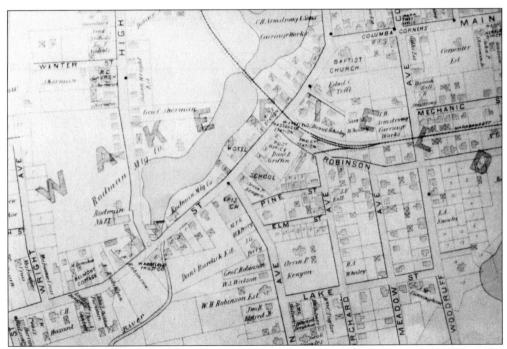

This map of Wakefield was made after 1876, when the Narragansett Pier Railroad was built. Many of the streets that now exist off Kenyon Avenue had not been platted at the time. You can use this map to find some of the houses in this chapter, as well as elsewhere in the book. (Courtesy Bob and Diane Smith)

This panorama of Wakefield looks across the Saugatucket River toward High Street. The spire of the first St. Francis of Assisi Church can be seen at left, and the Town Hall is the tallest landmark to the right. (Courtesy Pettaquamscutt Historical Society)

The South Kingstown Town Hall on High Street was built in 1877 as a gift to the town by Rowland G. Hazard. Designed by his son, also Rowland Hazard, and built by Kneeland Partelow, who built the Towers in Narragansett Pier, the Romanesque building retains its character despite a number of additions. (Courtesy Pettaquamscutt Historical Society)

Before the Wakefield Grammar School was built on this site in 1908, the fields by the Saugatucket River presented a pastoral scene. This view is looking north toward High Street. (Courtesy Pettaquamscutt Historical Society.)

Louis F. Bell, a contractor who built the Bell Block, The Pump House in Peace Dale, South County Hospital, and many other local buildings, is shown at center with his workers at a house on Upper Salt Pond, at what was then the Narragansett Country Club. (Courtesy Pettaquamscutt Historical Society)

This house on Winter Street is still standing, set off from the street. (Courtesy Everett Stedman)

Once the home of Deputy Gov. William H. Robinson, this home was built about 1720 on land Robinson purchased from his father, Rowland Robinson, who acquired it from the Narragansett Indians. Today it is the site of Shadow Farm. (Courtesy Pettaquamscutt Historical Society)

This photo of the Elisha A. Robinson House was taken in April 1866. (Courtesy Pettaquamscutt Historical Society)

This house, located off Post Road, is purported to be the birthplace of naval hero Oliver Hazard Perry, although historians differ on this. Some say Perry was born in the Judge Peckham House, on the Post Road southwest of Wakefield, while others claim he drew his first breath in a 2 1/2-story house in the Rocky Brook section of Peace Dale. This photo of what is sometimes called the Oliver Hazard Perry House was taken in May 1928. (Courtesy David Gates)

The Willard Hazard House, built about 1745 off Old Post Road on land that was part of the Pettaquamscutt Purchase, is believed by many to have been a stopover of George Washington when he traveled to Newport. In more recent years it was operated as "Ye Olde Tavern" by the Misses Reilly, who advertised in 1915: "Open day and evening . . . ice cream for sale . . . also—lunches put up for auto parties." The tavern was torn down in the late 1950s. (Courtesy Helen Farrell Allen/Tempus Fugit)

The residence of Mrs. George C. Robinson, which stood where the William Davis Miller House (now the Elks Lodge) is today on Main Street, was demolished in 1934. The house is Second Empire in style and was 2 1/2 stories. (Courtesy Bob and Diane Smith)

This is a view of Whitford Street, probably in the 1920s. Mr. and Mrs. George Smith lived in the white house to the left. (Courtesy Clinton Salisbury Sr.)

This house on Meadow Avenue, which is still standing, was home, at the time of this photograph, to Lillian Elnora (Tucker) Holley and her husband, George A. Holley. The Holleys would later buy Twin Chimneys at Dale Carlia Corner. (Courtesy Audrey Hosley)

W.B. Davidson, a popular landscape and portrait photographer in Wakefield, made this picture of the Daniel Whaley House. Whaley, who owned a large lot behind what is now the Weibel Block, built the house in 1887. (Courtesy Pettaquamscutt Historical Society)

The Brown family pose in front of their home at the corner of Robinson Street and Woodruff Avenue about 1915. They are, from left to right: daughter Ida and her nephew Jim; Elizabeth Brown, who died in 1916; and James Brown, who died in 1929. Elizabeth and James's son, Archie, was the Indian motorcycle agent for Wakefield. James Brown built the lot's distinctive wall of beach stones that he had carted from Point Judith. (Courtesy Everett Stedman)

The Wakefield train station, this house on the hill, and the Wakefield letters—all are gone from this spot, once known as Depot Square. The train station was located about where the Weibel Block is now. The house was home to Dr. Henry B. Potter. (Courtesy Peace Dale Library)

The Wakefield train station of the Narragansett Pier Railroad was demolished in April 1948. (Courtesy Peace Dale Library)

This view of Robinson Street shows the freight station (far right), the passenger station of the Narragansett Pier Railroad, and a business block (left) that was replaced by the Wakefield Post Office in 1936. (Courtesy Peace Dale Library)

This later view of Robinson Street, taken in 1933, shows the variety of businesses it held, from the Colonial Restaurant to dry goods. (Courtesy Donald and Shirley Southwick)

Members of the Welsh family pull away from Shadow Farm, a large estate on Silver Lake that included 70 acres with two houses. The estate dated to the Pettaquamscutt Purchase. The house shown here was begun in 1884 and added to and remodeled in 1904 by John L. Welsh of

Philadelphia. Beginning in 1979, the main house was turned into condominiums and new condos were built on the site. (Courtesy Pettaquamscutt Historical Society)

This is a last look at Wakefield from across the Saugatucket River, looking toward High Street. The first St. Francis of Assisi Church (note its spire) is no longer standing, but some of the houses on High Street are. (Courtesy Pettaquamscutt Historical Society)

Bibliography

The following reference materials were used in preparing this manuscript.

The Anchor, a South Kingstown High School publication, 1935.
The Cryptic, South Kingstown High School publication, June 1912 and 1922.
Gavin, Karen. "South County Hospital's Jubilee Year, 1919–1994." Supplement to *The Narragansett Times*, September 1994.
Jackson, Henry. "An Account of the Baptist Churches in Rhode Island, presented at the 28th Annual State Meeting of the R.I. Baptist State Convention, Providence, Nov. 8, 1853." George H. Whitney, Providence, 1854.
Lee, Virginia. "An Elusive Compromise: Rhode Island Coastal Ponds and Their People." Coastal Resources Center, University of Rhode Island, Marine Technical Report No. 73.
McNulty, Walter. "From Its First Chief: The History of a Police Department." *The Narragansett Times*, Oct. 8, 1964, p. 1.
The Narragansett Times: April 7, 1894; April 21, 1899; May 26, 1899; Oct. 13, 1899; June 22, 1900; April 13, 1906; June 8, 1906; April 12, 1918; April 16, April 30, July 16, Aug. 20, Aug. 27 and Oct. 29, 1920; April 11 and Oct. 24, 1924; March 15, May 17, Aug. 30 and Sept. 20, 1935; June 12 and Oct. 23, 1942; July 30, 1948; Aug. 11, 1955; March 14, Oct. 24 and Dec. 19, 1963; and Dec. 10, 1964.
Nebiker, Walter. "State of Rhode Island and Providence Plantations Preliminary Survey Report, Town of South Kingstown." Rhode Island Historical Preservation Commission, Providence, 1984.
Report of the School Committee of the Town of South Kingstown, 1895–96, 1896–97, 1906, 1907, 1914, 1915.
South Kingstown and Narragansett City Directory, 1910.
Stedman, Oliver H. *A Stroll Through Memory Lane*. Kingston Press, Vols. I–V, 1978.